Y0-AAQ-523

HOW TO TEACH YOUR CHILDREN ABOUT SEX...
without making a complete fool of yourself

BOOKS BY THE BERENSTAINS

How to Teach Your Children About Sex
Without Making a Complete Fool of Yourself

It's All in the Family

It's Still in the Family

Berenstain's Baby Book
Baby Makes Four
Marital Blitz
Lover Boy
Bedside Lover Boy
I Love You Kid, But Oh My Wife
Office Lover Boy
Have a Baby, My Wife Just Had a Cigar
What Dr. Freud Didn't Tell You
Flipsville-Squaresville
Mr. Dirty vs. Mrs. Clean
You Could Diet Laughing
Education: Impossible
Never Trust Anyone Over 13

CHILDREN'S BOOKS

The Big Honey Hunt
The Bike Lesson
The Bears' Picnic
The Bear Scouts
Inside Outside Upside Down
Bears on Wheels
Old Hat, New Hat
The Bears' Christmas

HOW TO TEACH YOUR CHILDREN ABOUT SEX...
without making a complete fool of yourself

IT'S POSSIBLE!

by Stan and Jan Berenstain

The McCall Publishing Company   *New York*

Published simultaneously in Canada by Doubleday Canada Ltd., Toronto.

Library of Congress Catalog Card Number 79-122114

SBN 8415-0039-8

The McCall Publishing Company
230 Park Avenue
New York, New York 10017

Printed in the United States of America

SOONER...

— THAT THERE IS SOMETHING
GOING ON THAT THEY
HAVEN'T TOLD HIM ABOUT
ON SESAME STREET · · ·

—AND HE WILL BEGIN TO ASK QUESTIONS!

SOME PARENTS, RECOGNIZING THE FIRST SIGNS OF SEXUAL AWARENESS, AND UNDER-STANDING THE KEY IMPORTANCE OF EARLY SEX ATTITUDES ON THE CHILD'S ENTIRE FUTURE LIFE · · ·

COMPLETELY!

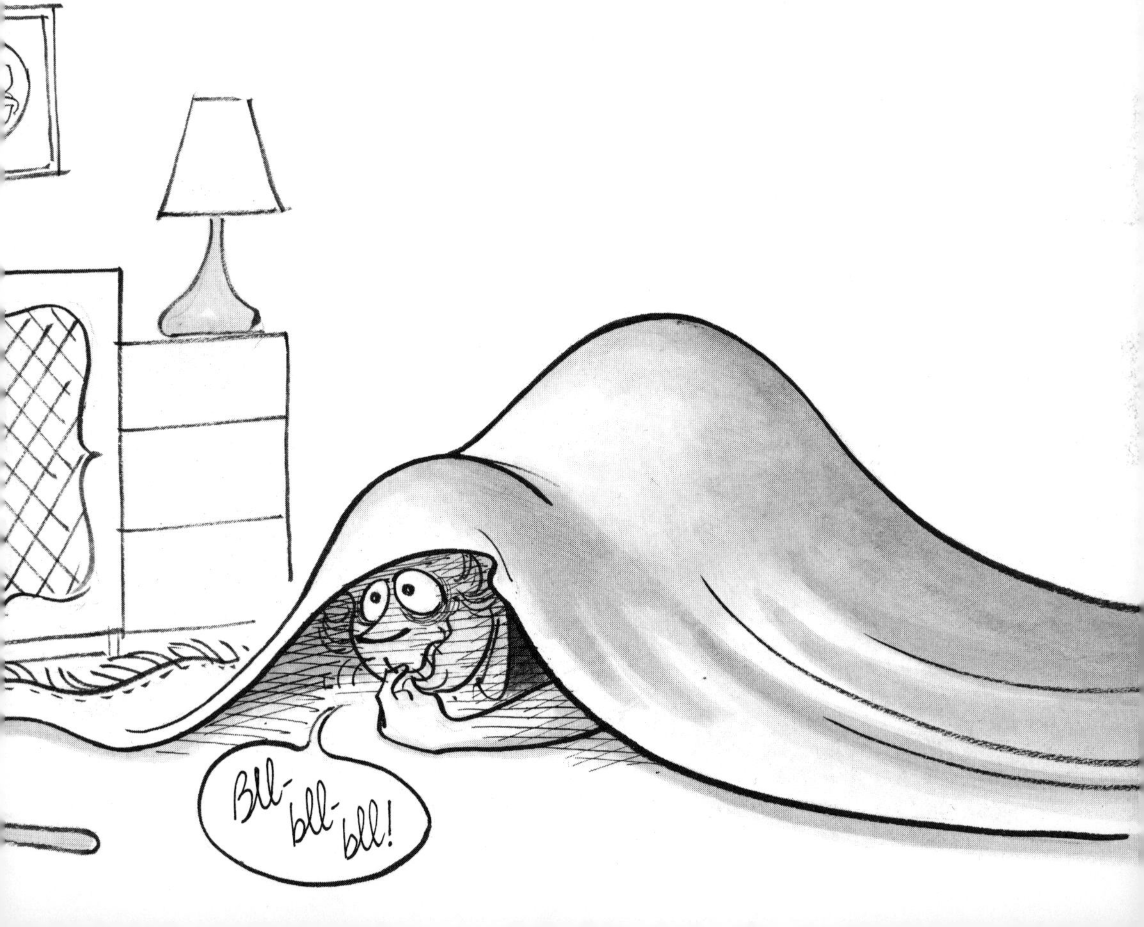

OTHER PARENTS ARE BETTER PREPARED. THEY HAVE ANTICIPATED THE DAY WHEN JUNIOR WOULD BEGIN "ASKING QUESTIONS" AND ARE READY WITH "ALL THE ANSWERS"...

— CAUSING <u>JUNIOR</u> TO FREAK OUT COMPLETELY.

A MORE SENSIBLE APPROACH IS TO STEER A MIDDLE COURSE AND ANSWER THE CHILD'S QUESTIONS AS SIMPLY AND STRAIGHTFORWARDLY AS POSSIBLE.

AFTER A CERTAIN AMOUNT OF EXPERIMENTING, THE CHILD WILL BEGIN TO ATTEMPT TO RELATE HIMSELF AND HIS NEWLY UNDERSTOOD SEXUAL IDENTITY TO THE LARGER WORLD · · ·

Daddy horses?
YES!
Daddy elephants?
YES!
Daddy rhinos?
YES!
Daddy dinosaurs?
YES!

YES!
YES!
YES!
DADDY TIGERS?
YES
DADDY BIRDS?
DADDY GORILLAS?
YES!
YES!
DADDY CHICKENS?
YES!
DADDY PIGS?
YES!
YES!

AS THE CHILD STRUGGLES TO IMPROVE HIS SMALL GRASP OF NATURE'S GRAND SCHEME HIS QUESTIONS BECOME MORE <u>DIFFICULT</u> . . .

WHICH BRINGS US, IN THE NICK OF TIME, TO THE <u>VITALLY</u> <u>IMPORTANT</u>, <u>MUCH</u> <u>PUBLICIZED</u>, <u>HIGHLY</u> <u>CONTROVERSIAL</u> QUESTION OF · · ·

...IN THE SCHOOLS!

MOST RELIABLE SURVEYS INDICATE THAT A LARGE MAJORITY OF PARENTS WELCOMES THE SUPPORT OF A WELL-DESIGNED SCHOOL SEX EDUCATION PROGRAM. BUT, EVEN WITH THIS BROAD BASE OF SUPPORT, EDUCATORS KNOW THAT NO MATTER HOW THEY APPROACH THE PROBLEM OF INTRODUCING SEX EDUCATION IN THE SCHOOL · · ·

— WHETHER IN OPEN FORUM WITH ALL CARDS ON THE TABLE · · ·

—IS GOING TO
FREAK OUT
THE LITTLE RED SCHOOLHOUSE
RED-TAINTED RAW SEX
TAUGHT HERE
IMPEACH EVERYBODY
STAMP OUT FILTH

BUT, SINCE EXTREME OPPONENTS
TEND TO STIMULATE EXTREME **PRO**PONENTS,

—AND SINCE EXTREMES TEND TO CANCEL EACH OTHER OUT, EDUCATORS ARE LEFT FREE TO GET ON WITH THE JOB— WHICH, IT CANNOT BE STRESSED TOO STRONGLY, IS ESSENTIALLY A JOB OF EDUCATION · · ·

— AND, AS SUCH, A LOT MORE <u>LIKE</u> OTHER EDU-
CATIONAL JOBS THAN DIFFERENT. WE ARE, AFTER
ALL, DEALING WITH · · ·

A GROUP OF TEACHERS

— SOME BAD · · ·

— SOME GOOD · · ·

- BUT MOSTLY AVERAGE,

A SET OF STUDENTS

–BUT MOSTLY AVERAGE·,

AND,

A BODY OF KNOWLEDGE – A BODY OF
KNOWLEDGE WHICH MAY BE DIFFICULT AND
CHALLENGING – BUT WHICH, NEVERTHELESS, MUST
BE TRANSMITTED THROUGH TRADITIONAL TOOLS AND
TECHNIQUES –THROUGH TEXTBOOKS, FOR EXAMPLE.

PUBLISHERS HAVE POSITIVELY OUTDONE THEM-
SELVES IN PROVIDING SEX EDUCATION PROGRAMS
WITH LIVELY AND INTERESTING TEXTS · · · ·

- RANGING FROM THE HIGHLY CREATIVE, RICHLY IMAGINATIVE · · ·

SO SAMMY AND HIS FRIENDS DECIDED TO LEAVE THEIR COZY HOME IN THE GONADS

—TO THE STARKLY CLINICAL . . . .

FEMALE CHICKEN

MALE CHICKEN

BUT WHETHER IT IS A SEX ED CLASS OR A CLASS IN ORIGAMI, KIDS ARE STILL KIDS, AND ANY GIVEN CLASS WILL INCLUDE CERTAIN CLASSIC TYPES . . .

THE KID WHO JUST CAN'T SEEM TO GET THE HANG OF IT,

THE KID WITH A REAL FEELING FOR THE SUBJECT,

-THAT GRAND LITTLE KID WITH A GENUINE
THIRST FOR KNOWLEDGE.

BUT, SEX EDUCATION IN
THE SCHOOLS IS NOT ENOUGH · · · ·

EDUCATORS ARE THE FIRST TO ADMIT THEY CANNOT DO THE JOB ALONE. THEY ARE IN ALMOST UNANIMOUS AGREEMENT THAT THE VERY INTIMATE QUESTIONS AND CURIOSITIES ARE BEST HANDLED ON THE HOME FRONT.

IF THE CHILD IS UNABLE TO GET THE HELP HE NEEDS FROM LOVING, SENSITIVE, OPEN PARENTS · · ·

SOME MORE
CONTEMPORARY-MINDED
PARENTS FEEL THE
MOST DIRECT WAY TO
ENGENDER A
HEALTHY, OPEN

ATTITUDE TOWARD
THE HUMAN BODY AND
SEX GENERALLY IS TO
MAINTAIN A CASUAL
ATTITUDE TOWARD
NUDITY IN THE HOME . . .

—GIVING THE CHILD NO CHOICE BUT TO LEAVE HOME.

SOME PARENTS TRY TO SOLVE THE PROBLEM OF ANSWERING REALLY DIFFICULT QUESTIONS ABOUT THE ULTIMATE SEXUAL EQUATION BY TAKING THE CHILD ON FIELD TRIPS TO · · ·

MUSEUMS · · ·

THE ZOO···

A NEARBY FARM · · ·

– IN THE HOPE THAT JUNIOR WILL BE ABLE TO PUT ONE AND ONE TOGETHER AND GET THREE.

SOME CHILDREN, HOWEVER, ARE UNABLE TO ACCOMPLISH THE NECESSARY IDENTIFICATION TO BENEFIT FROM THIS SORT OF EXPERIENCE · · ·

PARENTS OF LITTLE GIRLS ARE FACED
WITH A MORE DIFFICULT PROBLEM · · ·

— THE SENSE OF LOSS

— THE SENSE OF
DEPRIVATION

IN SUCH SITUATIONS, REINFORCEMENT OF THE MOTHER-ROLE IDENTIFICATION USUALLY RESTORES CONFIDENCE.

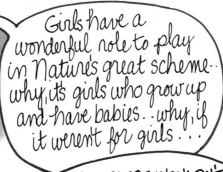

Girls have a wonderful role to play in Nature's great scheme.. why, it's girls who grow up and have babies.. why, if it weren't for girls...

..AND THERE WOULDN'T BE ANY PEOPLE 'CAUSE WE HAVE WONDERFUL SECRET PLACES IN OUR BODIES SO WE CAN HAVE BABIES AND BOYS CAN'T - SO WHO NEEDS BOYS - SO THERE!